For Matthias Anjoh Wehrle (1973–2012) —T.J.

To Stephen C. Sillett and Marie E. Antoine,
explorers and protectors of old-growth forests —W.M.

Sequoia

TONY JOHNSTON

Paintings by
WENDELL MINOR

A NEAL PORTER BOOK
ROARING BROOK PRESS
NEW YORK

Mornings
he stands
with a thin
shawl
of sun upon
his shoulders.

He watches the
grove below
slowly
fill with
light.

He watches the
clearing
quietly
fill with
deer.

He watches the
sky
burn blue at
the rim.

He holds out
his ancient
arms
and gathers
owls to him.

Springtimes,
clothed in his old man's
robes—
every shade of green—
he listens to
the thaw, to
waters
flow
again.

He listens to
beetles
scratch, to
woodpeckers
tap, to
firs converse
in wind.

As he listens
he stretches
his ancient
arms
and gathers
clouds to him.

He listens to
the sound of
one bee
hum.

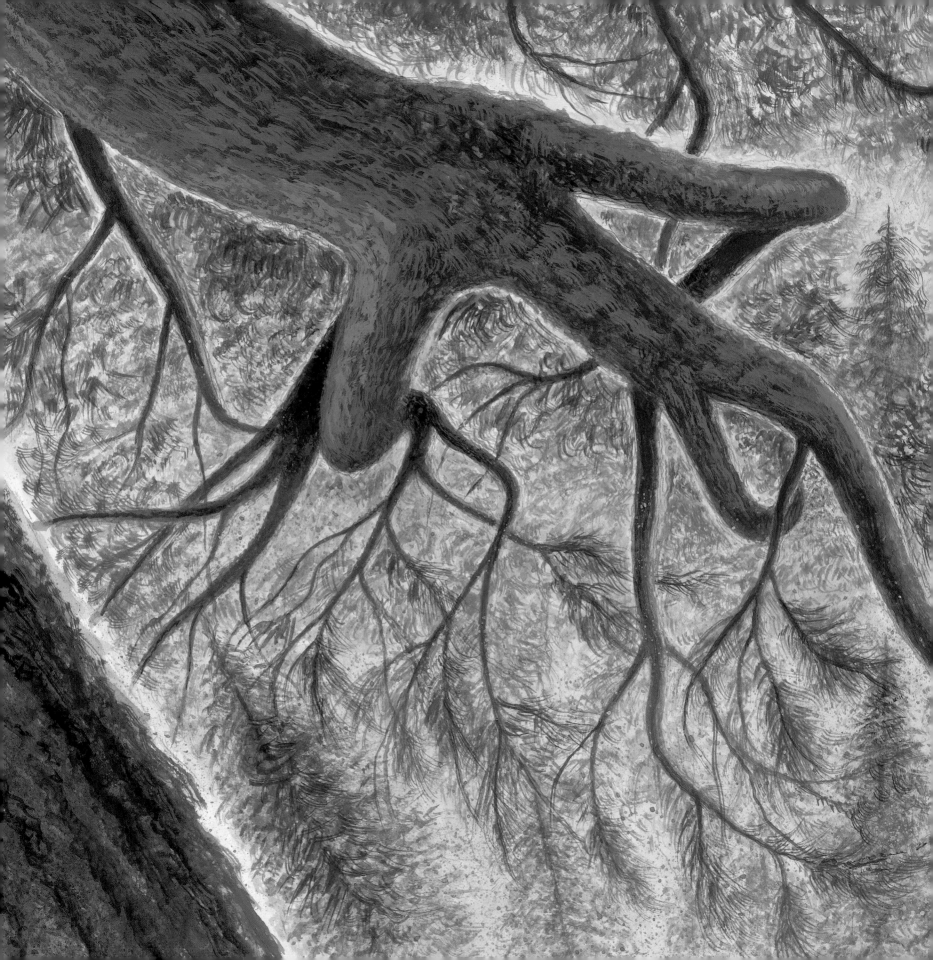

Summers,
from his post
above lower
trees,
he sniffs the
breeze.

Sometimes
he smells the very
heat,
shimmering
everywhere.

Sometimes
he smells the gray
of a sudden storm
in the air.
Then
he swirls into a dripping
cape of rain
and waits
for choirs of
frogs to
sing.

Sometimes
he smells fire.
He spreads
his ancient
arms
and gathers
flames to him.

Autumns,
among shifting drifts of
leaves,
he feels
a chill entering
his bones.

He feels
the pull of buried
dens lost
among
the hills.

He feels
the long year slip
away—
a wolf
down a wooded
path.

He feels
in his ringed
heart
the earth grow
still.
The birds
depart leaving him
alone.

He opens
his ancient, brittle
arms
and gathers
one last crow.

Winters
he waits for
something
in the forest's great
hushed
halls.

While he waits he
counts all
the moonrises he has
known, all
the centuries, all
the dawns,
until

snow
falls.

He
touches
snow.

Snow touches him.

Then bearded
and cloaked
and wild with
white,
he is
Merlin.

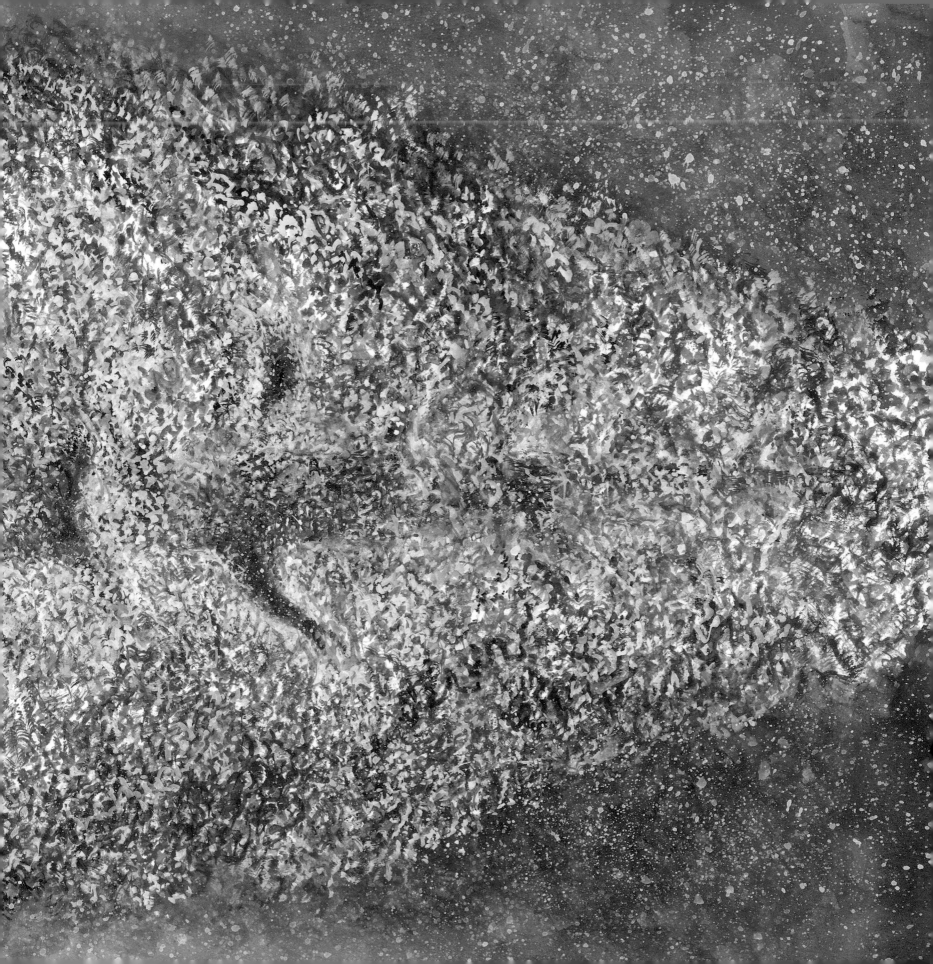

He throws wide
his ancient
arms
with joy
and gathers
snow to him.

Evenings
he gazes at sunsets
dwindling,
stares into the
glow, tells a tale
or two
to cedars
clustered there.

He tells of golden
grizzlies—
gone.

He tells of olden
forests—
gone.

He tells of golden
men.

Then he reaches
high his ancient
arms
and gathers
stars to him.

Some Notes on Sequoias

Giant sequoias and coast redwoods are often confused with each other or thought to be the same tree. Both are evergreen conifers of the cypress family. They are related to the dawn redwood, called "the living fossil," for it was only in 1944 that a live example was found in Moudao, China.

Sequoias, the oldsters, live for about 3,200 years. Redwoods, young whippersnappers, maybe 2,200. The giant sequoias' bark can be three feet thick; the puny redwoods' a mere one foot. The leaves of the sequoia have a "rat-tail" look, while the redwood's are feathery. Redwoods grow

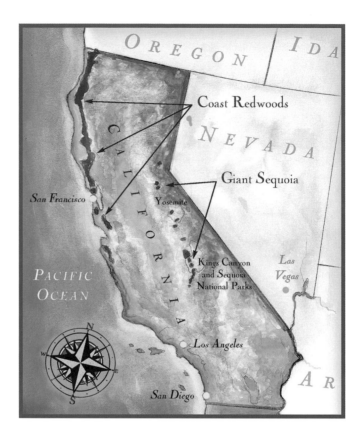

taller, but sequoias are bulkier. With a distance around the base of 102.6 feet and a volume of 52,500 cubic feet, the grand old man, General Sherman sequoia, is one of the largest living things on earth.

The range of sequoias is the western side of the

379 ft   311 ft

Tallest Redwood   Tallest Giant Sequoia

Sierra Nevada. They are mountain trees, snow trees, winter-loving beings that rely on snowpack and rain for water. Redwoods live in the "fog belt" of the California coast, getting water from coastal moisture. Both species host myriad living things—bugs, bats, butterflies, birds, blooms—amongst their canopies.

Global warming and the possibility of some future unknown disease or pest are the biggest threats to these trees. What once happened to our climate in 100,000 years is now happening in 200. In their foggy home, redwoods are safer. But because of their location, sequoias are at great risk. If the region warms and the snowpack dries up, the giants will die. Jim Folsom, director of the Gardens at the Huntington in San Marino,

California, believes that sequoias are in danger of extinction—that the day will come when we have to water them to keep them alive.

For now, they are protected from logging and other human harm in Sequoia, Yosemite, and other national and state parks. And if we all do our part, perhaps we can slow larger changes that put these giants and their "tenants" in peril. For when they are gone, like the golden grizzly of California, they will be forever gone. We cannot afford to lose them, not a one. Apart from providing shade for young trees and homes for other creatures, each is a magnificent poem that makes us look up in wonder at the beauty and majesty of Nature.

I would especially like to thank Neal Porter for his editorial prowess, Wendell Minor for his luminous paintings, and Jim Folsom for his genius in helping me understand the amazing creature, sequoia.

—T.J.

BIBLIOGRAPHY

RESOURCES

Folsom, James P., director of Huntington Botanical Gardens, conversations, 2012 & 2013.

Preston, Richard. *The Wild Trees: A Story of Passion and Daring*. New York. Random House, 2007.

FOR YOUNG READERS

Buff, Mary & Conrad. *Big Tree*. New York: The Viking Press, 1950.

Chin, Jason. *Redwoods*. New York: Roaring Brook Press, 2009.

A Neal Porter Book

Published by Roaring Brook Press

Roaring Brook Press is a division of Holtzbrinck Publishing Holdings Limited Partnership

175 Fifth Avenue, New York, New York 10010

The art for this book was created using gouache watercolor on Strathmore 500 Bristol.

mackids.com

Library of Congress Cataloging-in-Publication Data

Johnston, Tony, 1942- author.

   Sequoia / Tony Johnston ; illustrated by Wendell Minor. — First

edition .

    pages cm

  "A Neal Porter Book."

  ISBN 978-1-59643-727-2 (hardcover)

1. Giant sequoia—Juvenile poetry. 2. Trees—Juvenile poetry. 3.

Children's poetry, American. I. Minor, Wendell, illustrator. II. Title.

  PS3560.O393S47 2014

  811'.54—dc23

               2013044239

Roaring Brook Press books may be purchased for business or promotional use. For information on bulk purchases please contact Macmillan Corporate and Premium Sales Department at (800) 221-7945 x5442 or by email at specialmarkets@macmillan.com.

First edition 2014

Book design by Wendell Minor and Jennifer Browne

Printed in China by South China Printing Co. Ltd., Dongguan City, Guangdong Province

10   9   8   7   6   5   4   3   2   1

ARTIST'S ACKNOWLEDGMENTS

The artist wishes to thank Stephen C. Sillett and Marie E. Antoine of Humboldt State University for the generous use of their upper story photographs of the amazing giant sequoias and redwoods. They bravely climb these giants to unlock the secrets of the old-growth forest. Thanks also to Richard Preston, author of *The Wild Trees: A Story of Passion and Daring*, who gave me insight into all the wonderful work that Sillett and Antoine have been doing for many years. You can find more information about them and their work at: humboldt.edu/redwoods/sillett/